Samo Kreutz

# *Not Empty-Handed*

Haiku translation into English: Samo Kreutz, Alenka Zorman.
ISBN: 978-81-19654-03-1

First Edition: 2024
Rs. 200/-

Cyberwit.net
HIG 45 Kaushambi Kunj, Kalindipuram
Allahabad - 211011 (U.P.) India
http://www.cyberwit.net
Tel: +(91) 9415091004
E-mail: info@cyberwit.net



Printed in India at Repro.

*r*obin's departure …
on the cushioned stool
father's absence

*Milk moustache*

*s*tamp album …
from the opening page
a nightingale's song

*a*lbum za znamke
sredi začetne strani
slavčeva pesem

*b*etween
sleep and wakefulness –
an early spring woods

*b*lue hour
I silently follow
a daffodil smell

*w*ater rabbit
all those holes
inside us

*d*iscussing
about the meaning of life
a walk to the store

*t*haw …
seeping into the ground
the raven's shriek

*t*hin fog
the sun pierces
even my worries

*b*rushing teeth
she rinses her mouth
with a lark song

*t*he steps
yet to be taken –
a kindergarten

*c*hemistry kit
in a child's test tube
chamomile scent

*p*hone call …
this brief conversation
with a seagull

*f*irst spring visit
she shows her flat
to the violet scent

*w*indmills …
my wristwatch alarm
on snooze

*p*lanting seeds
all the career plans
of a little boy

granny and grandson
sown in the garden
their quality time

watering flowers
all the new shoots
of her stories

baking cookies …
a girl adds to the list
a new profession

*m*idtown park …
all differently coloured
birds

*f*lower therapy
completely calm
spring wind

*y*ellow carnations
that child's question
about begging

*s*nowdrops …
his first appointment
at a rehab centre

*a* pee stop
time to admire
daisies

*p*ost office
on the weighing scale
a hortensia scent

*w*isteria shadow
that letter she keeps
reading

*a*fternoon nap …
the serene face
of a scarecrow

*f*inch’s song …
a nearby skyscraper
overcrowded

*f*orget-me-not
he tells his mother
about her first date

*c*oughing …
stuck in the throat
a buttercup scent

*b*edtime kiss
now on mum's cheek
milk moustache

*t*his narcissus …
only in her dreams
grandmother

*c*ity school
paving the access
shrieks and drawings

*š*ola med bloki
dohod k njej tlakujejo
vzkliki in risbe

## *Dog and the rainbow*

*h*uge van
in the co-driver's seat
a dog and the rainbow

*o*gromen kombi
na mestu sovoznika
pes in mavrica

*p*regnant woman
that very first kick
of the haiku

*t*raffic jam...
even his watch
stopped

*s*hop queue
I let the bird singing
go first

*b*irth preparation
in her thick manual
a daisy

*w*orld’s fair
the toddler presents
newly learned word

*r*ose seedlings
multiplied so rapidly
grandson's questions

*m*agic act
those big tears
disappeared

*c*ircus show
throughout the arena
a child's babbling

*f*erocious lion
even her worries
frightened

*c*aged tiger
in the child's eyes
not behind bars

*c*hickadees flock
the art of counting
mastered

*l*ookalikes …
that parrot's eyes
in his mirror

*f*ull-time mum
under her care –
ducklings

Sunday noon
doing math together
teddy bear and me

hamster …
those big wheels
of his boyhood

her medicine
its main side effect
grandson's curiosity

*l*ilies scent
interrupted for a while
the school fight

*n*eighbour dispute
the loudest of us all
a cricket

*c*olourful kite
so close to the sun
boy's shouts

*r*euse centre
that mesmerizing
eyes

*t*ryst …
fondling her hair
a swallow shadow

*s*peechless …
all those words
in the meadow

*r*ipe strawberries
that detailed description
of his girlfriend

*r*ejection letter
back to square one
for a hot chocolate

*m*isty hills
another change
in his career

kissed
and embraced –
her lucky coin

butterfly wings
the day she proposed
to him

church bells ringing
falling out of the sky
raindrops

*a*dventure calls …
going on foot all the way
to the second floor

*h*iking jacket …
the Mt. Blanc smell
in my pockets

*C*amino talk
that unstoppable urge
to buy a sleeping bag

*l*ost luggage
redundant somewhere else
his carefreeness

*w*hale safari
that warm feeling
of his wife's breath

*g*reat outdoors
we tell each other stories
summer breeze and me

*e*nd of Camino
not in the photo
a new self

*h*ome again
that trip memento
her baby

*f*ootprints
this short stay
of my lullaby

*a*rt gallery …
in the golden frame
a whisper

*e*xhibition …
the greatest masterpiece
his wife

*y*ard work
where the weed grew
a cicada's chirp

linking
robin and lark song –
the manure smell

ruffle dress ...
how the daylight
plays tricks

bread oven …
that browned crust
of her hands

*w*eedy field …
the long talk about
his drinking

*s*trike …
all the seeds
that burgeoned

*o*vercooked …
the distinct smell
of his divorce

*d*issection …
that girl talk
about exes

*l*eaf pile
in the middle of it
young mushrooms

*g*rmada listja
sredi nje razraščeni
šopi mladih gob

# *The smell of soil*

*n*ut cracker
in a wide opening
the smell of kernels

*l*esen terilec
v široki odprtini
vonj po orehih

*t*igerlike…
chasing the shadows
a playful kitten

kid's bed
a thousand ways
to disappear

plate armour …
a small girl asks
about bullying

her dress …
the perfume scent
unzipped

*c*ommencement
already at the lectern
the ant

*c*ity mouse
not the same as before
this Aesop's fable

*b*achelor party
a different appearance
of the sun

*s*econd hand store
entering it hurriedly
the wind

*p*re-election rally
all the transformations
of a cloud

*b*reath vapour
the oak branches
severely crooked

leaf- raking …
the way she hides
her age

ripe apple
all the sweetness
of our silence

Potemkin Village
so carefully adjusted
his wig

*s*witching clothes
only in the mirror
an old woman

*a*geing …
bluebird shadow
grey

*d*ental visit …
even the light has
its own teeth

*r*eturning home
in her thin pochette
a rainbow

*e*vacuation drill
the first one outside
a housefly

*h*eavy frost …
if only he knew
how to listen

*a*valanche …
that one redundant
deed

*H*alloween moon …
wearing its own mask
her illness

*w*aiting room …
the body language
so loud

*m*edical record
carefully attached
the sage smell

*c*hurch window
a blurred reflection –
her prayer

*s*parrows flock
the first long walk
after his stroke

*g*ardening …
the smell of soil
in our words

*c*onquered peak
how quickly it slips
into the sunset

*e*arly evening
that long shadow
of the bell sound

*s*now smell …
her first visit to mum
in a nursing home

*c*aterpillar …
those last moments
as a male

*b*efore
becoming my shadow –
dad

*o*ld sweater
just a bit stretched
her mum's scent

*g*irl's tea party
waiting for grandad
his chair

*c*hrysanthemum
in every petal rests
different tale

*m*ockingbird …
she tells her children
the grandad's stories

*b*eech wood
at the foot of the stack
the pear tree shadow

*b*ukova drva
ob vznožju skladovnice
zgolj senca hruške

*Crystals in her hand*

*s*torage hall
among the bags of cement
the dawn shimmers

*s*kladiščna hala
med vrečami cementa
se lesketa zor

*f*rosty morning
the heavy silence
cracked

*J'accuse …*
that crow's echo
in my dream

*t*orn
among rosehip bushes
an eagle's cry

*c*limate changes
only her hair
white

*y*ear of the rabbit
he fills yet another
big hole

*o*ld bakery
smelling heady
the fog

*s*treet food …
the hawker serves me
a raindrop

*c*hurch entrance
waiting for Mass to begin
the frozen puddles

*a*nniversary
crystals in her hand –
first snowflakes

*l*icking icicle
the size of toddler's
smile

winter visit
not empty-handed –
the blizzard

high energy costs
the different shades
of snow

december sun
pleasantly warm
the quietness

*s*now drift …
that dance invitation
she never took

*m*elting icicles
he waits for a friend
to come out

*s*now shovelling
how the right words
reappear

*f*rozen river …
her attempt to talk
about the ex

*f*riendly dog
all that playfulness
at the cemetery gates

*w*inter half-light
the time we play
god

*n*ew shoes
on lacquered toecap
the old moon

*f*inally home
a much wider smile
in my father's photo

*C*hristmas Eve …
talking to the stars
an orphan

*e*mbers …
immediately warmer
the gaze

*c*old evening
smiling to him
the face in a coffee

*m*eteor shower
all the brightness
of a haiku

*s*nowy sunset …
in the maternity ward
festive ditty

*t*oddler's hand
no more waning
this moon

*o*ld fishing photo
that story how he tried
to win her

*g*rowing dusk …
where the keys were
his kitten's purr

*F*riday evening
fondling her gently
the bath water

*b*oy's gaze
inside his little house
the Big Dipper

*n*ew glasses
an old lady reads
the stars

*l*ate night snack
that daily portion
of news

*l*ittle doll …
this shooting star
in her eye

*s*nowmelt …
quenching the thirst
a hyacinth scent

*s*trong thaw
a broken house and snow
together melt away

*m*očna odjuga
skupaj s snegom pobira
scefrano hišo

## A WORD OR TWO ABOUT THE AUTHOR

Samo Kreutz lives in Ljubljana, Slovenia. He began to write as an eight-year-old boy, when he wrote his first story (and later a poem). One day his parents told him that simply by writing he cannot earn enough for a decent life, so he replied that he will become a writer and a joiner. Now, at the age of forty-nine, he is not yet a joiner (nor a carpenter), but the Bachelor of Economics, who besides poetry and short stories, also writes novels and haiku (since 2011). He is the author of ten books in Slovene (all published by the Ekslibris, publishing house in Ljubljana) and four in English (they are haiku books; the last two are titled *No Bigger Than a Crumb* and *Forgotten for a Moment*, all published by Cyberwit.net). His work has appeared in various Slovenian literary magazines, anthologies, on national Radio, on several international websites, e- and printed journals (most recently in the *Failed haiku – a journal of English Senryu*, and in the *Lothlorien Poetry Journal*).

## A NOTE ABOUT THE BOOK

*Not Empty-Handed* consists of 155 haiku. The poems in this collection reflect our lives and everything that marks them. They capture moments until something happens that disrupts and breaks down the established rhythm, so these verses also express themes of mourning, resignation, and ultimately, resilience in standing back on our own two feet. They are joined by poems with a touch of nature, so that new meanings or new contrasts could be established. The majority of these haiku can be found (in English, Slovene or both versions) in printed journals: *Better Than Starbucks: Poetry and Fiction Journal*, *Kingfisher Journal, Lothlorien Poetry Journal*, *Seashores: Haiku Journal*, and *Taj Mahal Review*, on websites: *Akita International Haiku Network*, *Ariel Chart: international literary journal, Asahi Haikuist Network*, *Autumn Moon Haiku Journal*, *Cattails: A Journal of the United Haiku and Tanka Society*, *Cold Moon Journal*, *Creatrix Haiku and Poetry Journal*, *First Literary Review – East*, *Green Ink Poetry, Ink Sweat & Tears: The poetry and prose webzine*, *Jalmurra: Art and Poetry Journal*, *Locutio*, *Poetry Pea*, *Scarlet Dragonfly Journal*, *Stardust Haiku Online Journal*, *The Bamboo Hut, The Big Windows Review, The Haiku Foundation (Haiku Dialogue), The Heron's Nest,* and *Wales Haiku Journal*, in anthologies: *Haiku zbornik: Ludbreg*, *Pesem si: zbornik*, *Samoborski haiku susreti Darko Plažanin*, and in quite a few broadcasts on the national Radio.

# CONTENTS

www.ingramcontent.com/pod-product-compliance
Lightning Source LLC
Chambersburg PA
CBHW050024170726
48282CB00025B/536
* 9 7 8 8 1 1 9 6 5 4 0 3 1 *